Rich Entertainment Group   John & Claire Caudwell
Viertel Routh Frankel Baruch Group Chunsoo Shin/Waxman-Dokton Broadway Across America

By special arrangement with Bubbles Incorporated, S.A. & Roy Export, S.A.S.

PRESENT

CHAPLIN
THE MUSICAL

BOOK BY
Christopher Curtis & Thomas Meehan

MUSIC & LYRICS BY
Christopher Curtis

INTRODUCING
ROB McCLURE
AS "Charlie Chaplin"

STARRING

Jim Borstelmann Jenn Colella Erin Mackey
Michael McCormick Christiane Noll
Zachary Unger Wayne Alan Wilcox

WITH

Justin Bowen Emilee Dupré Sara Edwards Leslie Donna Flesner Lisa Gajda Timothy Hughes
Ethan Khusidman Ian Liberto Renée Marino Michael Mendez Sarah O'Gleby
Hayley Podschun Adam Rogers William Ryall Eric Santagata Emily Tyra

SET DESIGN	COSTUME DESIGN	LIGHTING DESIGN	SOUND DESIGN	VIDEO/PROJECTION DESIGN
Beowulf Boritt	**Amy Clark** **Martin Pakledinaz**	**Ken Billington**	**Scott Lehrer** **Drew Levy**	**Jon Driscoll**

WIG/HAIR DESIGN	MAKE-UP DESIGN	CASTING	VOCAL & DIALECT COACH
Paul Huntley	**Angelina Avallone**	**Telsey + Company** **Patrick Goodwin, C.S.A.**	**Beth McGuire**

PRODUCTION STAGE MANAGER	PRESS REPRESENTATIVE	COMPANY MANAGER
Kim Vernace	**Boneau/Bryan-Brown**	**Bruce Kagel**

TECHNICAL SUPERVISOR	FLYING EFFECTS	GENERAL MANAGER
Chris Smith/Smitty	**Flying by Foy**	**Roy Gabay Productions**

MUSIC DIRECTOR/ VOCAL ARRANGEMENTS	ORCHESTRATIONS	MUSIC COORDINATOR	DANCE ARRANGEMENTS
Bryan Perri	**Larry Hochman**	**Howard Joines**	**Bryan Perri & Christopher Curtis**

ASSOCIATE PRODUCERS
Richard & Emily Smucker
Jon Luther

DIRECTED & CHOREOGRAPHED BY
Warren Carlyle

World Premiere of "Chaplin" produced by La Jolla Playhouse
Christopher Ashley, Artistic Director & Michael S. Rosenberg, Managing Director
Originally presented in the 2006 New York Musical Theatre Festival
The producers wish to express their appreciation to the Theatre Development Fund for its support of this production.

ISBN 978-1-4803-3245-4

HAL•LEONARD® CORPORATION
7777 W. BLUEMOUND RD. P.O. BOX 13819 MILWAUKEE, WI 53213

In Australia Contact:
Hal Leonard Australia Pty. Ltd.
4 Lentara Court
Cheltenham, Victoria, 3192 Australia
Email: ausadmin@halleonard.com.au

Visit Hal Leonard Online at
www.halleonard.com

OVERTURE

By CHRISTOPHER CURTIS

segue

LOOK AT ALL THE PEOPLE

Words and Music by
CHRISTOPHER CURTIS

Simply, quietly, rolling forward

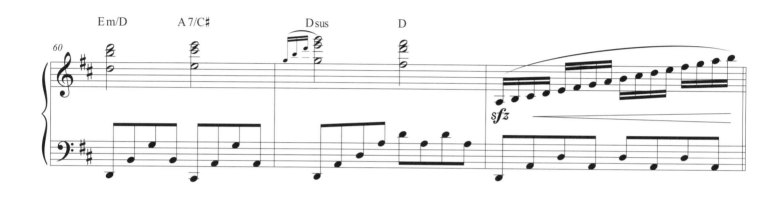

WHATCHA GONNA DO?

Words and Music by
CHRISTOPHER CURTIS

get your-self___ out of here!"?___ What-cha gon-na paint when you

can-not paint the town? Re - mem-ber, what-cha give is what al - ways goes a - round. And

what - cha gon - na do when it all falls down?

MC: *Ladies and gentlemen, Charlie Chaplin.*

Tempo di drunken

What-cha gon-na do when it all falls down and where ya gon-na go from

What-cha gon-na do when it all falls down and where ya gon-na go from

What-cha gon-na do when it all falls down and where ya gon-na go from

What-cha gon-na do when it all falls down and where ya gon-na go from

IF I LEFT LONDON

Words and Music by
CHRISTOPHER CURTIS

CHARLIE:
If I left Lon - don to - mor - row, would I find gold __ in the west?

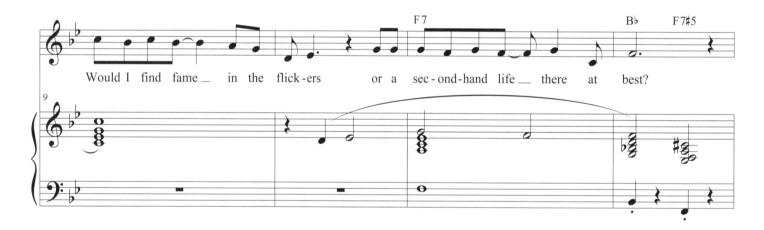

Would I find fame __ in the flick - ers or a sec - ond-hand life __ there at best?

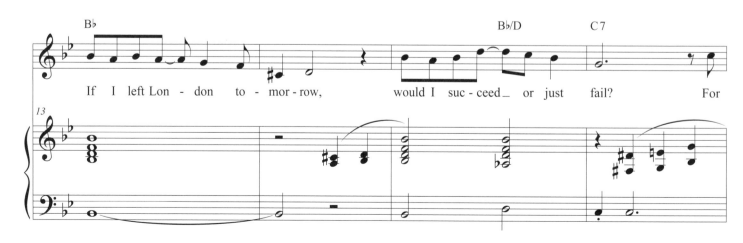

If I left Lon - don to - mor - row, would I suc - ceed __ or just fail? For

SENNETT SONG

Words and Music by
CHRISTOPHER CURTIS

SENNETT: *All right, let's get started.*

Fast Soft-shoe

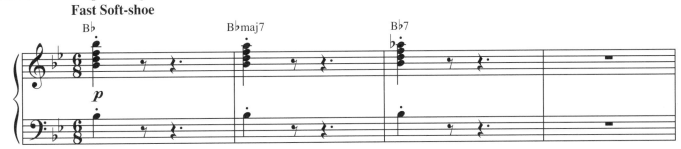

All you have to do is follow my direction. Got it!

CHARLIE: *I guess so. But*

who are all these people, I don't know any of them.

SENNETT: That's

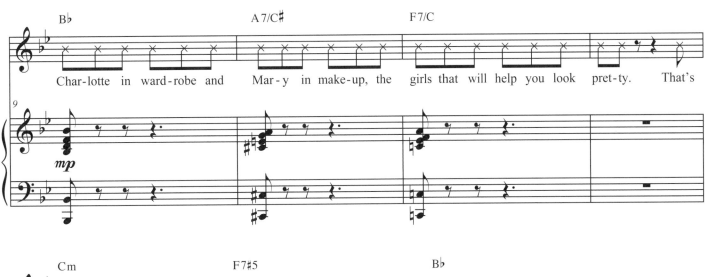

Char-lotte in ward-robe and Mar-y in make-up, the girls that will help you look pret-ty. That's

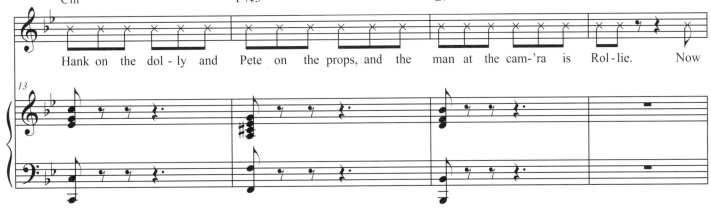

Hank on the dol-ly and Pete on the props, and the man at the cam-'ra is Rol-lie. Now

D7 D7/F♯ Gm Gm/B♭
Cue the cops and cue the pies and vil - lains hid - den in dis - guise.
65
C7 C7/E F Gm7 G♯dim7 F/A
Chap - lin, help me, time is mon - ey. Won't you show me some-thing fun - ny?
69
B♭ B♭maj7 B♭7 G+
Ma - bel's sweat - ing, Fat - ty's thin - ning, just give me a gag that's win - ning.
73
Cm Cm(maj7) Cm7 F+(add2)
Rol - lie's roll - ing, Pete is wait - ing, move it, kid, stop hes - i - tat - ing.
77

Fat -ty in the face. I know it's schtick, I know it's crude, but

who can real - ly blame us? So, come on, kid, and show me now the

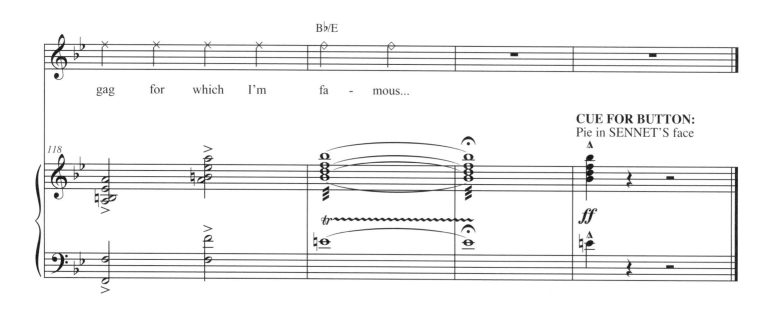

gag for which I'm fa - mous...

CUE FOR BUTTON:
Pie in SENNET'S face

TRAMP SHUFFLE PT. 1

Words and Music by
CHRISTOPHER CURTIS

SENNETT: *And what would you call this…?*
CHARLIE: *Character.*

SENNETT: *Ah, yes, you got me there. Character.*
CHARLIE: *He's a poet. A dreamer. A wanderer.*

CHARLIE: *A tramp.*
SENNETT: *A tramp? I like the sound of that.*

SENNETT: *But what's his, you know…?*
CHARLIE: *Motivation?*

Faster

shuf -fles.

SENNETT: *Cut! Perfect!*

shuf - fle.

USHER:

Come see___ Char - lie Chap - lin play - ing here___ at the Strand.

Come see___ Char - lie Chap - lin, first time___ in the land.

segue

TRAMP SHUFFLE PT. 2

Words and Music by
CHRISTOPHER CURTIS

SENNETT: *What do you hear, Charlie?*
CHARLIE: *Laughter, Mr. Sennett. What do you hear?*

SENNETT *: Money, Charlie. Lots and lots of money.*

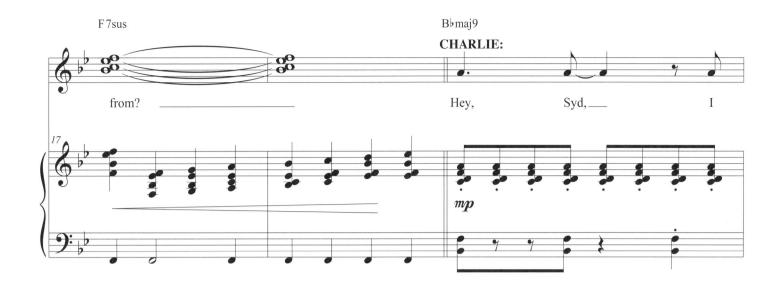

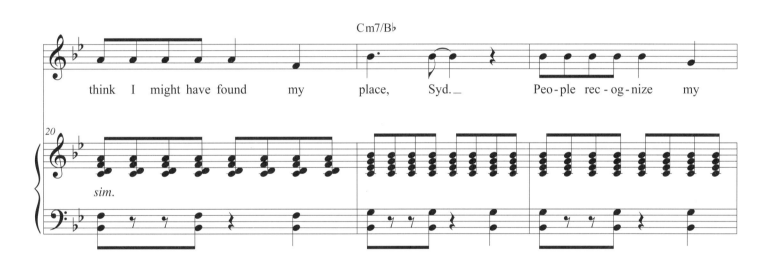

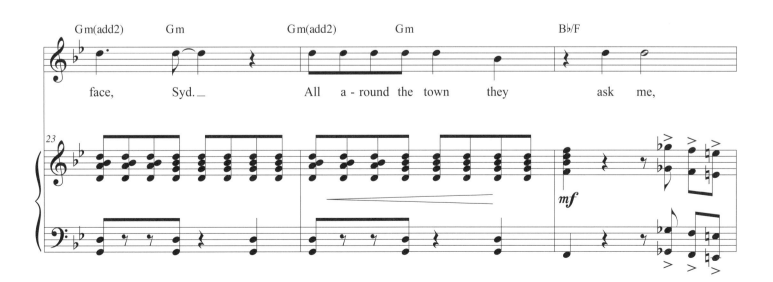

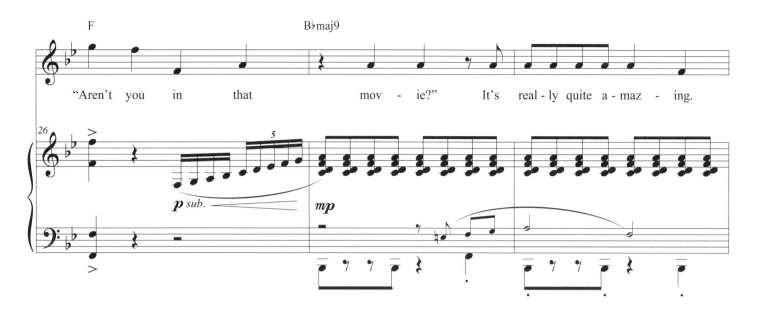

"Aren't you in that mov - ie?" It's real - ly quite a - maz - ing.

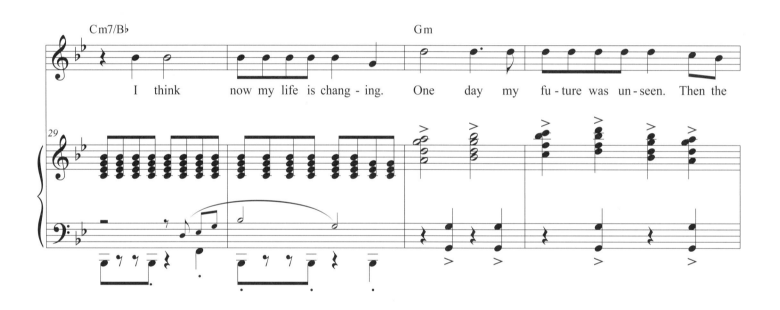

I think now my life is chang - ing. One day my fu - ture was un - seen. Then the

next day my name's up - on the screen. And hey, Syd,— I think I've fi - n'lly found my

44

Shimmering, whimsical, with drive

JUST ANOTHER DAY
IN HOLLYWOOD

Words and Music by
CHRISTOPHER CURTIS

lights are al-ways glow-ing and the cam'ra's al-ways roll-ing. The di-rec-tor's al-ways shout-ing, "Just one

CHARLIE: *Just one more!*

more!"

Ah.

Ah.

Star - lets al - ways gaz - ing at the lead - ing man who's play - ing, who is

ALF: *Modern Times! Factory Scene, Take 58!* **CHARLIE:** *Conveyor belt, go!*

hop - ing that he's bet - ter than be - fore

HEDDA: *Hello, I'm Hedda Hopper and this is Hedda Hopper's Hollywood.*

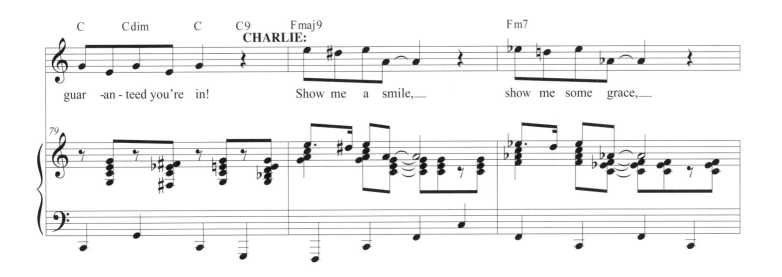

THE LIFE THAT YOU WISHED FOR

Words and Music by
CHRISTOPHER CURTIS

HANNAH: *"But he was there that night. Were you?"*   **HANNAH:** *"Whatever happened*
CHARLIE: *"Yes, I was."*   *to that boy who sang with me?"*

Like sunshine through a window pane, glassy

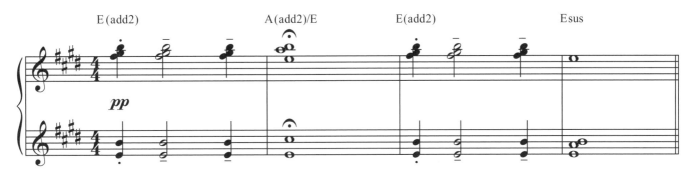

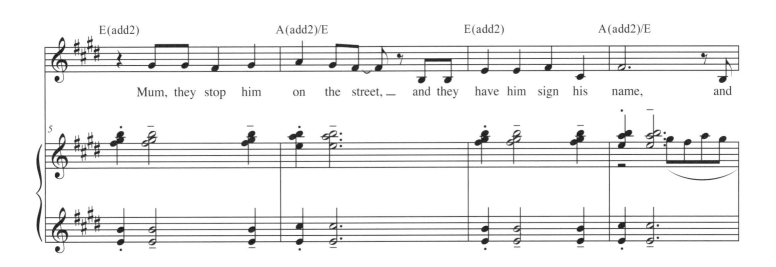

Mum, they stop him on the street, — and they have him sign his name, and

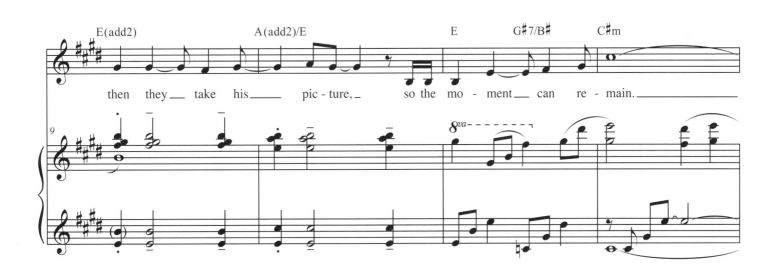

then they — take his — pic-ture, — so the mo-ment — can re-main. _____

WHEN IT ALL FALLS DOWN

Words and Music by
CHRISTOPHER CURTIS

Hey, there,____ Mis-ter Chap-lin,____ you may think I'm____ rath-er small____ 'cause the

posh pap - ers are fall - ing at your feet.____ So,

go a - head____ and snub me,____ and don't re - turn____ my call,____ and

minimal minimal

66

THE MAN OF ALL COUNTRIES

Words and Music by
CHRISTOPHER CURTIS

CHARLIE (VOICE OVER): *I am not a Communist, I am a humanist, a man of all countries, who cares deeply for all of those whom the world has oppressed and forgotten.*

WHAT ONLY LOVE CAN SEE

Words and Music by
CHRISTOPHER CURTIS

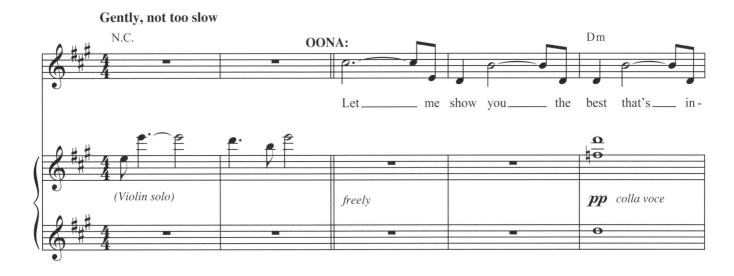

Gently, not too slow

Let _____ me show you _____ the best that's in-

side you. Leave the films be- hind you _____ just stay and talk to me. The

Simply

tramp _____ can charm me with a look that may be fun- ny, but

WHERE ARE ALL THE PEOPLE?

Words and Music by
CHRISTOPHER CURTIS

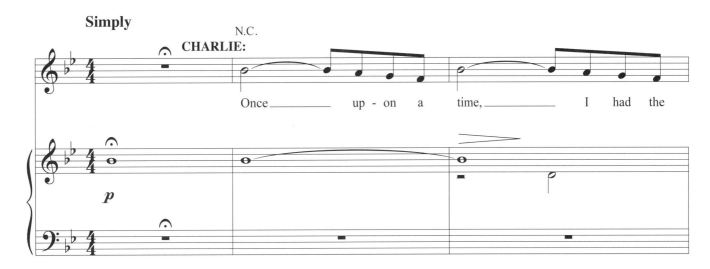

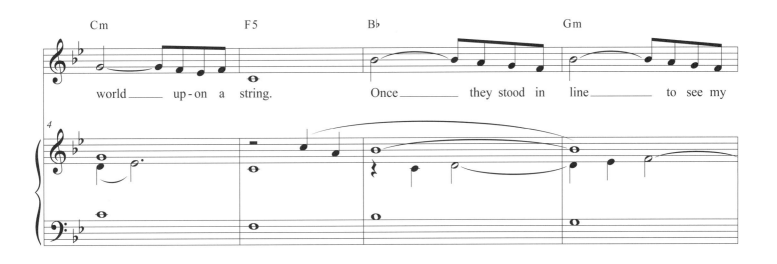

WHAT ONLY LOVE CAN SEE
(Duet Version)

Words and Music by
CHRISTOPHER CURTIS

OONA: *Yes, the world loved the tramp, but you are who I love.*

Gently, not too slow

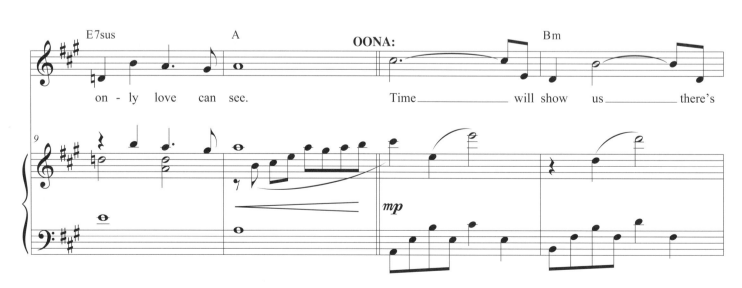

THIS MAN

Words and Music by
CHRISTOPHER CURTIS

Moderately flowing

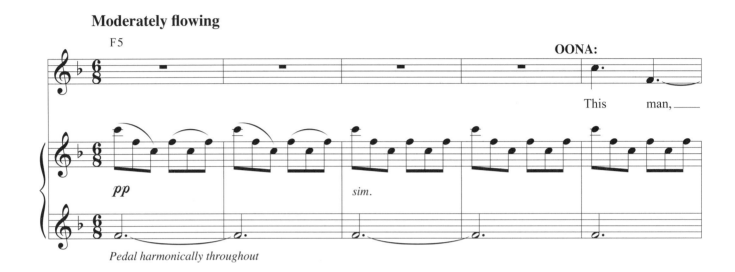

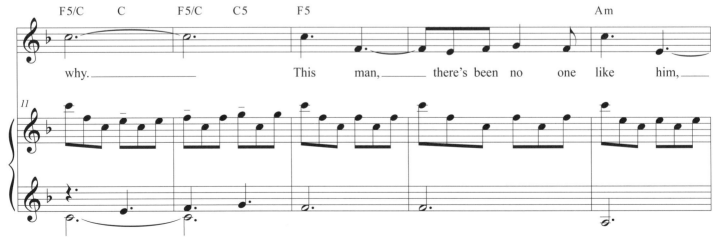

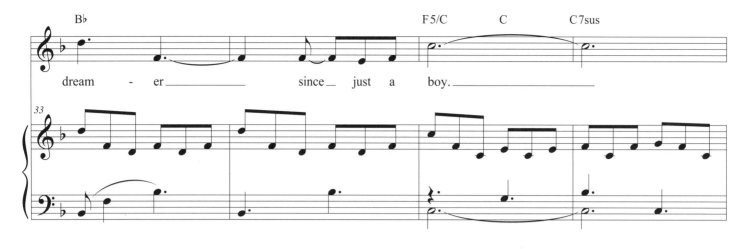

dream - er_____ since just a boy._____

This lit - tle child_____ who
This life,_____ so full of heart - ache,_____ but

cried_____ that night,_____
one life_____ gave_ so much joy._____